End Time Revelation

Apostle Ruben A. Martinez

End Time Revelation

By Apostle Ruben A. Martinez

Copyright © 2024 by Apostle Ruben A. Martinez

ISBN: 978-1-61529-206-6

Vision Publishing
P.O. Box 1680
Ramona, CA 92065
1 800 – 9 –VISION
www.booksbyvision.org

All scriptures are taken from the NKJV unless otherwise noted.

Dedication

This book is being dedicated to God the Father, and the Son, and the Holy Spirit. I will now begin to journey into the End Time Revelation from the Father, the Son, and the Holy Spirit.

Preface

The purpose for writing this book is to wake up the church to an understanding of the end times so that the believer can seek the heart of the Father.

Today we have a lot of people calling themselves prophets, but who have not been tested or tried. Matthew 7:15 reads, "Beware of false prophets, which come to you in sheep's clothing, but inwardly they are ravening wolves." This is what we have today.

In 2 Timothy 2:15, it reads, "Study to shew thyself approved unto God, a workman that needeth not to be ashamed, rightly dividing the word of truth."

My prayer is that the church will submit to the will of God to get end time understanding.

Table of Contents

Part 1 - Introduction

God has asked me to write about the end times to bring an understanding to what it means. I trust that God will guide me in the writing of this book. It is with great joy that I take this task knowing that I must trust in God, to give me all the understanding that I am going to need to write this book.

"And when the people were gathered thick together, He began to say, this is an evil generation they seek a sign, and there shall no sign be given it, but the sign of Jonas the prophet." (Luke 11:29) Jesus knew how and what would bring a multitude together. They were seeking a sign, and Jesus knew just how to answer them, and it was a shocker. Jesus had the right answers for them.

Here we have Jesus telling the people that they will get no sign, but that of a prophet. They were seeking a sign from heaven that they could identify with the time of the coming of the Messiah. Jesus takes them to the Old Testament so that they won't miss what He is saying to them. Jesus tells them that they are an evil generation. "For as Jonas was a sign unto the Ninevites, so shall also the Son of man be to this generation." (Luke 11:30)

Jesus tells them that Jonah was a sign to the Ninevites and that the Son of man is the sign to this generation. Why was Jesus telling them this? So that they would have the understanding that He was greater than Jonah the prophet?

"For as Jonah was three days and three nights in the whale's belly, so shall the Son of man be three days and three nights in the heart of the earth." (Matt 12:40) The answer is that the resurrection of Christ from the dead will be greater than that of Jonah the prophet. Christ was telling them that signs were granted to those who desired them for the confirmation of their faith. Abraham and Gideon were granted signs because of their faith but signs were denied to those who demanded them for the excuse of their unbelief. Jesus was telling them that they would get a sign of a different kind from all the others. The resurrection of Christ from the dead, by His own power, would surpass the rest. The resurrection of Christ would be the sign of Jonah to them. Jesus tells them that Nineveh repented at the preaching of Jonah, and "…behold, a greater than Jonah is here." (Matthew 12:41) Jesus is greater and now there are more prophets today than any time in history, and there are more apostles today than any other time. The prophets are sounding the trumpet now more than any other time in the history of the church and the Bible. This is the greatest time for the fulfillment of the prophetic word of God.

When revelation comes it produces understanding of what God is revealing to the person who is getting the revelation. End time revelation is going to be needed to discern this revelation that is being spoken of today. Many are prophesying that we are at the end but what end are they prophesying about? No one should be prophesying anything of which they have no understanding. Studying the word of God will help us to have the understanding that is needed for these times that we are in. There is no greater understanding than the understanding of the Old Testament that will lead us to understand the times that we are faced with today. Revelation will produce understanding of what the end will be and when it will begin to take place at the time that God reveals it. We must remember that all is in God's timing, which is perfect timing. The timing of man is always off. There are many different views that have been taught on end time revelation.

The book of Revelation is the prophecy of Jesus Christ. The Spirit of Jesus gives the prophecy to John to write. John is the son of Zebedee and the brother of James. There are many different views and teachings about end time revelation, and a lot of books have been written about it over the years. I must say that there have been some good books that have been written. It is most important that the times that we are in be understood. There must be a lot of prayer to get the impartation of what the Lord wants to reveal to His prophets and to His apostles. The church is at its best time in history because God is moving, and the church needs to be moving in the direction that God is moving. It's time for the church to awaken.

Part 2 - Messianic Christology

Daniel's Prayer – 9:3-19

Daniel's detailed prayer can be divided into two portions. The first (verses 3-14) is the confession of sin. Daniel acknowledged both sin and guilt which had been incurred in two ways: first by disobedience to the Law of Moses, and second by disobedience to the prophets who came after Moses. Daniel neither denied the sin of his nation nor his sin; by the pronoun "we" Daniel fully identified with all Jewish people in their sins. He did not see sin as merely a bad habit, but as something ingrained in the people that had brought on divine judgment. This disobedience to both the law and the prophets caused Israel "confusion of face," an idiom which literally means a sense of shame. It also resulted in the need for forgiveness. Here Daniel confessed that to God belongs forgiveness and mercy, and that forgiveness was needed. Daniel concluded the first part of his prayer by describing the punishment for sin and guilt. That punishment, captivity in Babylon, confirmed the words of the prophets who had predicted it and confirmed the Law of Moses which taught that divine judgment would come as a result of disobedience.

The second part of the prayer (verses 15-19) is a plea for mercy. Daniel made his plea on the basis of righteousness – not Israel's, but God's righteousness. He also pleaded for mercy on the basis of God's grace. Israel did not merit mercy, but the grace of God was, and is, able to extend it anyway. Furthermore, the righteousness of God required

Him to fulfill His promises, and therefore He should do so at the end of the 70-year period.

The conclusion of Daniel's prayer is very dramatic: "O Lord, hear! O Lord, forgive! O Lord, listen and take action! For Thine own sake, O my God, do not delay, because Thy city and Thy people are called by Thy name." When Daniel asks God to "not delay," he is asking God to count the 70 years from 605BC and not 597 BSc. or 586 BC.

The Arrival of Gabriel – 9:20-23

Then, while Daniel was presenting his supplications, he was interrupted. He apparently had intended to say more when Gabriel arrived. The interruption came "about the time of the evening offering." This refers to the daily, regular evening sacrifice that was offered while the Temple stood. Although it had not been practiced for seven decades, Daniel showed his longing for the return from captivity and for the rebuilding of the Temple by remembering the sacrifice. Gabriel told Daniel that the purpose of his visit was first, to correct Daniel's mis-understanding concerning when the Messianic Kingdom would be set up and to present God's revelation which contained a timetable for Messiah's first coming.

The Decree of the Seventy Sevens – 9:24a

Gabriel's prophecy to Daniel began with the words: "Seventy sevens have been decreed for your people and your holy city…" Many English versions have translated the phrase to read seventy "weeks." But this translation is not totally accurate and has caused some confusion about the meaning of the passage.

Most Jews know the Hebrew for "weeks" because of the observance of the Feast of Weeks, and that Hebrew word is Shavuot. However, the word that appears here in the Hebrew text is shavuim, which means "sevens." This word refers to a "seven" of anything with the context determining the content of the "seven." It is similar to the English word "dozen," which means twelve of anything based upon context.

It is obvious here that Daniel had been thinking in terms of years - specifically the 70 years of captivity. He had assumed that the captivity would end after 70 years and that the kingdom would be established after those 70 years. But here Gabriel was using a play on words in the Hebrew text, pointing out that, insofar as Messiah's Kingdom was concerned, it was not 70 "years," but 70 "sevens" of years, or a total of 490 years (70x7).

This period of 490 years had been "decreed" for the Jewish people and the holy city of Jerusalem. The Hebrew word translated "decreed" literally means "to cut off" or to "determine." In Chapters 2, 7, and 8, God revealed to Daniel the course of future world history in which Gentiles would have a dominant role over the Jewish people. This lengthy period began with the Babylonian Empire and was to continue until the establishment of Messiah's Kingdom. For that reason, it is often referred to as the Times of the Gentiles. Now the prophet was told that a total of 490 years was to be "cut out" of the times of the Gentiles. This 490-year period had been "determined" or "decreed" for the accomplishment of final restoration of Israel and the establishment of the Messiah's Kingdom.

The focus of the program of the Seventy Sevens was "your people and your holy city." The "people" were Daniel's people, the Jewish people, and "the city" was Daniel's city, Jerusalem. Although he had spent most of his life in the city of Babylon, Jerusalem was still Daniel's city. For Jews, whether they are in the land or outside the land, their city is always Jerusalem – not any other.

It is important to note that the program of Seventy Sevens does not concern the Gentiles or the Church; it concerns the Jewish people and the city of Jerusalem. The program of the Seventy Sevens, both the First Coming and the Second Coming of the Messiah, but it is primarily the First Coming that will be our concern here.

The Purpose of the Seventy Sevens – 9:24b

Next, Daniel was told by Gabriel that the Seventy Sevens are to accomplish six purposes. The first three are negative and undesirable elements which will be removed. The second three are positive and desirable elements to be affected.

The first Purpose is "to finish the transgression." The Hebrew word translated "to finish" means "to restrain firmly," "to restrain completely," or "to bring to completion." The Hebrew word translated "transgression" is a very strong word for sin and more literally means "to rebel." The Hebrew text uses this word with the definitive article, so the literal translation is "the transgression," or "the rebellion."

The point is that some specific act of rebellion is finally going to be completely restrained and brought to an end. This act of rebellion or transgression is to come under complete control so that it will no longer flourish. Israel's apostasy is now to be firmly restrained in keeping with a similar prediction in Isaiah 59:20. Specifically, this is the rejection of the Messiah as dealt with in Isaiah 52:13 - 53:12.

The second purpose of the Seventy Sevens is "to make an end of sin." The Hebrew word translated "to make an end" literally means "to seal up" or "to shut up in prison." It means "to be securely locked up, not allowed to roam at random." The Hebrew word translated as "sin" literally means "to miss the mark." It refers to sins of daily life, rather than to any specific sin. Even these sins are to be put to an end and taken away.

This, too, is quite in keeping with predictions by the prophets who proclaim that in the Messianic Kingdom sinning would cease from Israel (Isaiah 27:9; Ezekiel 36:25-27; Jeremiah 31:31-34).

The third purpose is "to make atonement for iniquity." The Hebrew word translated "to make atonement" is kaphar, which has the same root meaning as the word kippur, as in Yom Kippur, the Day of Atonement. The third purpose is to make sure the first two purposes will be accomplished: that of finishing the transgression and making an end of sin. The word translated "iniquity" refers to inward sin. This has sometimes been referred to as the sin nature, or perhaps a more common term among Jewish people would be yetzer hara, "the evil inclination."

The fourth purpose of the Seventy Sevens is "to bring in everlasting righteousness." This could be more literally translated "to bring in an age of righteousness" since the Hebrew word, "Olam" is better translated as "age" rather than as "everlasting."

This age of righteousness is to be the Messianic Kingdom spoken of in the Prophets (Isaiah 1:26; 11:2-5; 32:17; Jeremiah 23:5-6; 33:15-18). It is this very age that Daniel had been expecting to see established after the 70 years of captivity, but now he is told that they will only be after the 490-year period of the Seventy Sevens.

The fifth purpose is "to shut up." "To shut up" means "to cause a cessation" or "to completely fulfill." Thus, vision and prophecy are to be completely fulfilled. "Vision" is a reference to oral prophecy, while "prophecy" refers to written prophecy. Both oral and written prophecy, will cease with the final fulfillment of all revelations.

The final purpose of the Seventy Sevens is "to anoint the most holy place." This is a reference to the Jewish Temple which is to be rebuilt when the Messiah comes. It refers to the same Temple that Daniel's contemporary, Ezekiel, described in great detail (Ezekiel 40-48).

The Start of the Seventy Sevens – 9:25a

Daniel was clearly told when the Seventy Sevens would begin their countdown. Gabriel said, "Know and discern, that from the issuing of a decree to restore and rebuild Jerusalem…" Thus, the Seventy Sevens would begin with a decree involving the rebuilding of the city of Jerusalem. Not everything in Persian chronology is as clear as we would like to have it, and there are still some gaps in our knowledge of history. But from what biblical and historical records we do have, there are four possible answers to the question of which decree the passage refers to.

One is the Decree of Cyrus, issued somewhere between 538 - 536 BC, which concerned the rebuilding of the Temple (II Chronicles 36:22-23; Ezra 1:1-4; 6:1-5) and of the city of Jerusalem (Isaiah 44:28; 45:13). Another option is the Decree of Darius Hystaspes (Ezra 6:6-12), issued in the year 521 BC, which was a reaffirmation of the Decree of Cyrus. A third possibility is the Decree of Artaxerxes to Ezra (Ezra 7:11-26), issued in 458 BC, which contained permission to proceed with the Temple service. The last option is the Decree of Artaxerxes to Nehemiah (Nehemiah 2:1-8), issued in the year 444 BC. This decree specifically concerned the rebuilding of the walls around Jerusalem. Of these four possibilities, only the first and fourth decrees have any real validity in fulfilling the wording that Gabriel gave to Daniel. It is not necessary for our purpose here to deal with the various arguments of either option, but one thing that is certain is that by the year 444 BC the countdown of the Seventy Sevens had begun.

Unit 1: The First Sixty-Nine Sevens – 9:25b

The Seventy-Sevens are divided into three separate units: Seven Sevens, Sixty-two Sevens and One Seven. During the first time period of Seven Sevens, or 49 years, Jerusalem would be "built again, with a plaza moat, even in times of distress." The second block of time, Sixty-two Sevens, or a total of 434 years, immediately followed the first for a total of Sixty-nine Sevens, or 483 years. There is no implication of a gap of time between the first and second subdivision of the Seventy-Sevens.

It is at this point that we are told the ending point of the Sixty-nine Sevens is to be "until Messiah the Prince." As clearly as Daniel could have stated it, he taught that 483 years after the decree to rebuild Jerusalem had been issued, Messiah would be here on earth.

The obvious conclusion is this: if Messiah was not on earth 483 years after a decree was issued to rebuild Jerusalem, then Daniel was a false prophet, and his book has no business being in the Hebrew Scriptures. However, if Daniel was correct and his prophecy was fulfilled, then who was the Messiah of whom he spoke?

Unit 2: The Events between the Sixty-Ninth & Seventieth Seven - 9:26

Whereas the second subdivision of the Seventy Sevens was immediately to follow the first, the third subdivision was not immediately to follow the second. Daniel pointed out in verse 26 that three things would occur after this second subdivision ends and before the third one begins.

Stepping back in time and looking ahead from Daniel's perspective in verse 26, we see first, that "the Messiah will be cut off and have nothing." The Hebrew word translated "cut off" is the common word used in the Mosaic Law and simply means "to be killed." The implication of the term is that the Messiah would not only be killed, but also that He would die a penal death by execution.

The Hebrew expression translated "and have nothing" has two possible meanings. It may mean "nothingness," emphasizing Messiah's state at death. It can also be translated "but not for himself," and the meaning would then be that "He died for others rather than for Himself – a substitutionary death." The latter meaning would be much more consistent with what the prophets had to say about the reason for Messiah's death. (e.g., Isaiah 53:1-12)

The first three purposes of the Seventy Sevens: to finish the transgression, to make an end of sin, and to make atonement for iniquity- all have to be accomplished by some means of atonement. The Law of Moses decreed that atonement is made by blood. (Leviticus 17:11) It appears that Messiah's death, "not for himself" but for others, would be the means by which Israel's transgression, sin, and iniquity would be atoned for. The point of this phrase is that between the end of the second subdivision, the Sixty-ninth Seven, and before the start of the Seventieth Seven, Messiah would be killed and would die a penal, substitutionary death.

Second, during this interim period it would also happen that "the people of the prince who is to come will destroy the city and the sanctuary. And its end will come with a flood... "The city and Temple which were to be rebuilt because of the decree by which the Seventy Sevens began, would be destroyed; some time after the Messiah was cut off, Jerusalem and the Temple would suffer another destruction. Our knowledge of history during this period is extremely clear: the people responsible for this deed were the Romans; Jerusalem and the Temple were destroyed in the year 70AD. Based upon this verse, it is also clear that the Messiah should have both come and died prior to the year 70AD. If such an event did not take place, then Daniel was a false prophet. If such an event did occur, then the question must be answered, who was that Messiah who was killed before 70AD?

The third thing to take note of would be, "even to the end there will be war; desolations are determined." For the remainder of the interval between the Sixty-ninth Seven and the Seventieth, the land would be characterized by war and its resulting condition would be desolation. All this would set the stage for the final, or Seventieth-Seven.

Unit 3: The Seventieth Seven – 9:27

From where we stand in time today, the last 7 years of Daniel's prophecy are still future, but it is with their conclusion that all six purposes of verse 24 will reach their fulfillment. The main points of the verse are as follows: first the Seventieth Seven will begin only with the signing of a 7-year covenant or treaty between Israel and a major Gentile political leader. The pronoun "he" in verse 27 goes back to its nearest antecedent in the verse, which is not the Messiah but "the prince who is to come." This "prince" has been a topic of Daniel's earlier prophecies in chapters 7-8. This political leader is better known to Christians as the Antichrist.

Second, in the middle of the Seventieth Seven, that is, after 3½ years, this Gentile leader will break his treaty with Israel and cause a cessation of the sacrificial system. The implication here is that by this time, a Temple in Jerusalem will have been rebuilt; the sacrificial system of Moses will have been reinstituted, then be stopped by force.

Third, the result of the breaking of this covenant is that the Temple will now be abominated. The "abomination" refers to an image or an idol. Just as it was in the days of Antiochus Epiphanes, so it will be again in the future when a Gentile ruler will abominate the Temple by means of idolatry.

Fourth, the "abomination" is to be followed by wrath and desolation, persecution, and warfare for the remaining half of the Seventieth Seven, or the final 3½ years. This is similar to the trials and tribulations the rabbis spoke of as preparation for the establishment of the Messianic Kingdom. These terrible days were referred to as "the footsteps of the Messiah," and as "the birth-pangs of the Messiah." Once those days run their course, the last three things predicted in verse 24 will occur. The age of righteousness will be brought in; the most holy place will be anointed; and every vision and prophecy will be fulfilled. At this point the Messianic Kingdom for which the prophet Daniel yearned will be set up.

Obviously, the Messianic Kingdom requires the Messiah to rule as King. This means the Messiah will come after the Seventieth Seven. Yet earlier, Daniel stated that the Messiah would come and be killed after the Sixty-ninth Seven. This would appear to be a contradiction unless Daniel was speaking of two comings of the Messiah. The first time was to be after the Sixty-ninth Seven, when He would die a penal, substitutionary death for the sins of Israel and accomplish the first three purposes listed in verse 24.

The second time, still future, was to be after the Seventieth-Seven, when He will establish the Messianic Kingdom and accomplish the last three things of verse 24. There is also an important implication here that should not be missed: the Messiah would be killed after His First coming, yet He would be alive at His Second Coming. The implication is that the Messiah would be resurrected from the dead after He was killed.

Conclusions

This dramatic prophecy features certain things in very clear and unmistakable terms. First, the Messiah was to be on earth 483 years after the decree to rebuild Jerusalem. Second, after His appearance on earth, He was to be killed – not for His own sins, but rather for those of others – and the death He would die was to be the death of the penalty of the Law. Third, the death of the Messiah had to come sometime before Jerusalem and the Temple were destroyed again; this occurred in the year 70AD. Fourth, sometime after the destruction of Jerusalem and the Temple, and following a long period of warfare, the Seventieth Seven will commence.

Once that has run its course, Messiah's Kingdom and the age of righteousness will be established. For that to occur, the implication is that the Messiah who was killed would return again. But who is this Messiah? Only one man fulfills all that is required in this passage, Jesus of Nazareth. He was born into the Jewish world and proclaimed His Messiahship 483 years after the decree to rebuild and restore Jerusalem was issued. In the year 30AD Jesus was executed by crucifixion. Daniel indicated that He would be cut off – not for Himself, but rather for others. Isaiah 53 also prophesied the death of the Messiah, pointing out that He would die a substitutionary death on behalf of His people, Israel.

The teaching of the New Testament is that Jesus died a penal death by taking upon Himself the penalty of the Law as a substitute for His people. In keeping with Daniel 9:24, He died for the purpose of making an atonement for sins. Three days after His death, He was resurrected. Finally, the New Testament proclaims the fact that He will someday return to set up His kingdom and the age of righteousness. If Daniel was right, then Messiah came and died prior to the year 70AD. If Daniel was right, then there are no other options for who the Messiah is, Jesus of Nazareth. If Daniel was right, Jesus is destined to return and to set up the Messianic Kingdom. This information is from the book, *Messianic Christology* by Arnold G. Fruchtenbaum Th., M, Ph.D.

In my own studying I believe that the 69th week of Daniel ended when Jesus Christ went to the cross. I also believe that the 70th week of Daniel began the day that Jesus Christ went to the cross. It is very clear that the rebuilding of the wall was the fulfilling of the 69th week of Daniel. In my very own opinion, I believe that we are living in the 70th week of Daniel and have been for a very long time. I also believe that it is repeating. We have not seen the rebuilding of the third temple as of yet, and the antichrist has not been revealed.

Matthew 24

I believe that we are in Matthew 24 because all that is in this chapter is being played out right in front of our eyes. So, let's look at the scripture.

Verse: 6 "And ye shall hear of wars and rumors of wars: see that ye be not troubled: for all these things must come to pass, but the end is not yet."

Verse: 7 "For nation shall rise against nation, and kingdom against kingdom: and there shall be famines, and pestilences, and earthquakes, in diverse places."

In verses 4, 5, 11 and 24, Jesus talks about deceptions. There would be false Christs and false prophets. These people would show great signs and wonders, so much so that, if it were possible, even the very elect would be deceived. We are seeing this right now. It is right in our face and yet we do not believe what is taking place right now. We see the deceptions of world governments that have the people deceived. Governments that lie in order to stay in power and rule in deception. They want to make the people to depend on the government, which shows that the government does not depend on God. We can see the deception that is in the church. Pastors are deceiving the membership of the ministries which God has entrusted to them. They preach false teachings and make themselves as god over their congregation. There are pastors and ministries operating from a controlling spirit. Jesus warns us today just as He did back then of false prophets. There are many false prophets running around today. God is exposing false pastors and preachers that are in the pulpits. God is also exposing the false membership that is in His church. Just as it was back then, so will it be now. There are many prophecies that are being released today and many of them are not true.

In verses 5, 23 and 26 False Christs. Many false Christs are all over the place. The church does not even know how to identify them. The reason for this is because the church has been caught up in the false teaching. Who are these false Christs? They are the pastors and preachers. The congregants are equally false because they do not study the word of God.

Wars and rumors of wars. Wars have been going on for a very long time and the world has not ended. Let's look at some of the wars that have already taken place. World War 1 started on July 28, 1914, and ended on November 11, 1918. This was a global conflict between two coalitions, the Allies and the Central Powers. Battles took place throughout Europe, the Middle East, Africa, the Pacific, and parts of Asia. World War 1 started because of the assassination of Austrian Archduke Franz Ferdinand. Austria declared war on Serbia. The main cause of World War 1 was alliances between countries, militarism, nationalism, imperialism, secret diplomacy, and internationalism. The assassination of Archduke Franz Ferdinand, heir to the throne of Austria- Hungary, Gavrilo Principal in Bosnia is widely accepted as the starting point for World War 1.

World War 2 started in 1939 and ended in 1945 and was the deadliest and most destructive war in history. Before the war, Germany, America, and the rest of the world were going through the Great Depression. What caused World War 2? The War was caused by Adolf Hitler's invasion of Poland in September 1939, which drove Great Britain and France to declare war on Germany. The participants of World War 2 were Britain, France, Russia, China, and the United States. The major Axis Powers were Germany, Italy, and Japan.

The Korean War June 25, 1950 - July 27, 1953.

The Vietnam War 1964 – 1975.

The Desert Shield / Desert Storm 1990 – 1991.

America's Wars total 1775 – 1991.

Global war on Terror Oct 2001 – Sept 2021.

As we can see, wars have been with the world throughout history. This does leave out all the wars before the modern days of today. We need to have a better understanding of end time revelation.

While many are saying that we are going into World War 3, I believe that we are far from it. Yes, things that are taking place today point to Matthew 24, "And ye shall hear of wars and rumors of wars: see that ye be not troubled: for all these things must come to pass, but the end is not yet." (Matthew 24:6) Many are in error concerning the prophecies that have been released that do not line up with the word of God. Many do not study the scriptures in its proper context and full value and full volume. There are those who do not have an end time understanding at all.

Israel has always been in a war yet still exists today and is at war even now. Jesus tells us that these things must take place and that the end is not yet. We must be careful of what comes out of us. We have seen wars and heard of wars in different places throughout the world and the world has not ended. These things must take place.

At present, Russia and Ukraine are at war which started on February 20, 2014. On October 7, 2023, Israel and Hamas went to war. Again, this is not the end; it is the beginning of what is to come later. Jesus tells us not to be worried because these things must take place. Let's not leave the United States out of what is taking place, being involved by supplying weapons. China is not to be left out. China has a big part in what is happening right now.

Nation shall rise against nation, and kingdom against kingdom: and there shall be famines, and pestilences, and earthquakes in diverse places. So, let's look at causes of famines. Many famines are precipitated by natural causes, such as drought, flooding, unseasonable cold, typhoons, vermin depredations, insect infestations, and plant diseases. The most common human cause of famine is warfare, which destroys crops and food supplies and disrupts the distribution of food. We can see that famines have been around for a very long time.

Famine. Now let's see what the Bible has to say about famines. Famine was seen as both punishment and opportunity. Suffering opened the door for repentance and change. For example, when the famously wise King Solomon inaugurated the temple in Jerusalem, he prayed that God would be forgiving when, in the future, a famine-stricken Israel turns toward the newly built temple for mercy. God will get the attention of the world and the leaders of nations.

We have seen famines across different parts of the world. God has spared many different nations. God will always give warning first before He passes judgment. What is very sad is having the Bible but not reading it to learn the blueprint on how to prepare for what is coming? What has taken place already is repeating itself again. Many are not paying attention and the pulpit is at fault for not teaching how to prepare the congregants. It's time that the church wakes up. Many in the church do not even know how to evangelize. Many say that they are an Evangelist, but I don't think they are. I say this because they are not trained. Knowing they have a call is one thing; learning the office is another part of the call. Back in the Old Testament time kingdoms rose against kingdoms, and we see the same taking place once again today. I believe that teaching Matthew 24 in the churches and ministries and in Bible studies would be very helpful. Pestilence is a fatal epidemic disease especially the bubonic plague. Pestilence is referred to as the bubonic plague. It also refers to any other epidemic disease that is highly contagious, infectious, virulent, and devastating. The Egyptians' ten plagues should be an example for the world of today. So, we can see that famine and pestilence must occur.

Earthquakes. Let's look at some of the earthquakes that took place back in the beginning of creation. On the third day of creation, the waters of the earth were collected into oceanic basins as continents appeared. (Genesis 1:9-10) Before day three, the waters had been over the whole earth.

Continents seem to have been uplifted and the ocean floor was depressed during a great faulting process that established the "foundations of the earth." We are told that angels saw and praised the omnipotent God as the shaking process occurred. (Job 38:38 4-7; Psalm 104:4-6)

Noah's Flood. The year-long, global flood in the days of Noah was the greatest sedimentary and tectonic event in the history of our planet since creation. (Genesis 6-9) The destruction of Sodom and Gomorrah: A disaster called an overthrow was delivered in about 2050BC on the cities of Sodom and Gomorrah. (Genesis 19:24-28) Moses on Mount Sinai, Exodus 19:18. Korah's Rebellion, Numbers 16:1-40. These are just some of the earthquakes that took place during that time frame that was compartmentalized. In the past 40-50 years, our records show that we have exceeded the long-term average number of major earthquakes about a dozen times. The national earthquake information center says there are about 55 earthquakes a day around the world. That's 20,000 a year. Earthquakes NASA. As we can see, the Bible tells us that these things will take place. In the book of Matthew, it is clear that Jesus is giving the world a very clear picture that these events will take place, but that it is not the end. We know that these events took place already.

Cycles. Let's talk about Cycles. We must learn about the cycles of war in the Bible in order to understand the times that we are in right now. Without that understanding we will not have the true meaning of the wars that have been and the ones that are taking place right now. I believe that we are in a cycle right now, and many are saying that we are heading to World War 3. I believe that we are not. Many of the prophecies have not been completed. There is a lot that must take place that has not happened yet. God keeps the "natural" cycles recurring such as in the weather, for instance, as well as other cyclical events mentioned in chapter 1. There is security in knowing that a steady Hand rests on the helm – One that can be absolutely relied upon. (bibletools.org) God repeats Himself in the Bible so that we pay attention to the words and remember them and reflect on them.

Anti-Semitism. (Matthew 24:9) "Then shall they deliver you up to be afflicted and shall kill you: and ye shall be hated of all nations for my name's sake." (Mark 13:9) "But take heed to yourselves: for they shall deliver you up to councils; and in the synagogues ye shall be beaten: and ye shall be brought before rulers and kings for my sake, for a testimony against them."

Definitions from Oxford Languages, Anti-Semitism: hostility to or prejudice against Jewish people, "he is a leader in the fight against Anti–Semitism". As we can see in the scriptures, Jesus warned the Jewish people that they would face Anti-Semitism. The things that happened then are still happening and still exist today. We also exper-ience the Anti-Semitism against Christianity just as it was back then. So, nothing has changed since back then to right now in modern times. Anti-Semitism means hatred of Jews. The word first appeared in the 19th century when the classification of people into different races was considered normal. Many people in Europe thought that the white race was better than the other races. But do Jews belong to a separate race? And is Anti-Semitism racism? Racism is based on the idea that there are different human races: the white race, black race, the yellow race, and the red race.

People of a race are assumed to share certain characteristics. From the Anne Frank House, I believe that we need to be careful with the words Anti-Semitism and racism because they can be one and the same. These two words have had a part in keeping the human race apart for centuries. Thus, we can see that from the 19th century on these words have had much power in separating and keeping the human race apart. Classification, Anti-Semitism, and Racism play big roles in the lives of people today. It is right in our face, and we do not face up to it. We must fight back at what is keeping us apart. The world must repent from this sin that was created by words that have overpowered the human race.

Covid–19 Pandemic. The pandemic was created to eliminate and reduce the population. You have certain people who want to eliminate 7 billion people from the earth. The World Economic Forum, the World Health Organization and the United Nations are working together to eliminate the population.

Let me get back to Covid–19. The first thing the government did was close the church and many of the churches that closed have not been able to open up again. In my opinion this falls in line with Anti–Semitism against Christianity. The church did not fight back against the shutdown. Only two churches that are from California took the fight to the government and to the Supreme Court and won. This is what happens when you put your faith and trust in Jesus Christ. We must remember that all things are possible with God. It's time for the church to wake up and fight back; it can no longer keep silent.

I don't want to forget about Anti-Semitism in the church, this must be addressed as well. The different denominations are fighting against each other instead of working to help each other. The Church has the power in Jesus Christ. The church needs to fight against Anti-Semitism inside the church and outside the church. Can you imagine if Jesus Christ was Anti-Semitic against His own creation? We must fight the good fight against all this Anti-Semitism and all this hatred.

The biggest threat to the church today is herself. The reason why I say this is because of the false doctrine that is being taught today. The church cannot allow the unbeliever to dictate how the church is to teach. The church allowed the Obama administration and .03 percent to dictate to 97 percent of the nation that it was alright to allow two men to marry and two women to marry each other. This is Anti–Semitism against the church and 97 percent of the nation.

Let us look at what they are doing with our children, teaching them that it's alright to be gay and transgender. The schools are also teaching that our children do not have to identify themselves as a boy or a girl. Here you have the identity of children being stolen by the government. So here you have Anti–Semitism against the parents. Parents absolutely must fight against this identity theft that has been thrust upon our children and their parents. I also want to say that we do not know the horrors that parents face;

and children face when their parents disown them. This must be looked at and dealt with.

This must be taught in the church because it will not be taught in the schools. Parents can no longer be silent, the church and parents must come together as one and fight this attack on the lives of our children, our homes, and our churches. We are human beings created in the image of God. We must stand together with God and fight back against the devil. We must fight back against what the government is doing. This shows the Anti–Semitism that the government has against its own people and nation. Church, it is time to wake up!

Offenses. (Matthew 18:1-18) "At the same time came the disciples unto Jesus, saying, who is the greatest in the kingdom of heaven"? The answer that Jesus gave the disciples was that He wanted them to change their mind and put aside who was the greatest. Jesus was telling them that to be great, they would have to be like children. The reason why Jesus said this to the disciples was because children did not have any standing in society. This was a great teaching lesson that He taught His disciples. This does not exclude adults from this teaching; Jesus made this very clear to His disciples. The moral of this teaching is that those who teach, must teach to lead those that are like children to God. This also is the responsibility of those who are in government. Governments are to be held responsible for the teaching that they give to people. No one is excluded from this teaching. The biggest error that anyone can commit is to lead children astray from learning the law of the Bible. Parents, teachers, and governments that lead children and adults astray will be held accountable and responsible for their wrongdoing. In this era that we live in, wrong is right and right is wrong. It is time for the church to stop looking the other way. Our faith is in God not in man. For those that are called to teach and preach, must teach truth. The church must be really converted. The church must be of one mindset, and that is of the kingdom of God. The pride, ambition, and affection of honor and dominion which appear in you must be repented of and reformed. Many who say they are called of God are not, they are imposters.

Verse 7, "Woe unto the world because of offenses! For it must be that offenses come but woe to the man by whom the offense cometh!" This present world is an evil world. It is so full of sins, snares, and sorrows. In this verse we see the word woe twice in the verse, it refers to grief, anguish, wretchedness, calamity, or trouble. It can be used as an exclamation of judgment on others, misfortune on oneself, sadness over others, and may give way to forgiveness, comfort, and deliverance. (Quora.com) "Let us be careful of the offenses that come out of our mouths." Jesus said that it is not what goes in us but what comes out of us. There is a lot of room for us to repent as individuals, as church leaders, and as governments. Repentance brings restoration! The point that Jesus was making was that Christians were not to be gullible or naïve, but they need to look to God with trusting faith, and the acceptance of their own limitations. Those who guide other spiritual children are serving God. Those who lead believers astray can expect harsh judgment. God's way is the best way.

That is why we need Him to guide us when we need help. No one is exempt! This teaching of Jesus gives the Christian community life to live and be the salt of the earth and light of the world.

Verse 11, "For the Son of man is come to save that which was lost." It's time for the real church of the Lord Jesus Christ to show up and show out. So that the unbeliever can turn their lives to the Lord Jesus Christ. The church needs to be real to a lost world that is looking to be found. This is a very important time for the real Evangelist to go out and evangelize. This is a critical time! What will it take for the church to come together as one and fight the good fight? It's time to take back what the enemy stole. Let's get our children back in the church and those that are not and bring them in also.

We talk a lot and say that we are in the end times, so if this is the end times then we need to come together now. The truth is that the church is not ready for the end. I believe that we are coming to an end of an era of time where things are changing, that means that the church has to change its ways in order to move forward with the changes that God is making in this very hour. I believe that every pastor and minister should take the time to study Matthew 18!

Betrayals. Verse 9, "Then shall they deliver you up to be afflicted and shall kill you: and ye shall be hated of all nations for my name's sake." (Mark 13:12) "Now the brother shall betray the brother to death, and the father the son; and children shall rise up against their parents and shall have them to be put to death. When a nation betrays

God and betrays the people of God, then their own relations shall betray them."

Politics play a very big role in betrayals by selling the people out to the corporations of the world. They get together and plot what will be their next move. They plot in their beds at night where they think that no one is watching them or hearing them. These people are corrupt to the very core. Not only them, but the church is corrupt and the pulpit. Many lies come from the media and from the highest office in the nation. This corruption is very deep. Corruption has always been around; this is not new.

When they were crucifying Jesus Christ they were throwing dice on His prayer shawl. So, when we see what is being done today right in our face and we don't say anything, we deserve everything that they are doing because we are not fighting back. For being a believer and preaching the Kingdom of Jesus Christ we are being put in jail all over the world. Christians are being killed in many parts of the world, but we don't hear them saying anything or writing anything about it. What was done back then is being done today right in our face.

Brother shall betray the brother to death, the father the son and children against their parents, we see this every day. Children killing their parents and parents killing their children. Parents and children committing suicide on a daily basis, thinking that they have nowhere to turn.

What will it take for the church to wake up? Let's look at what God has put in the church. He has put doctors, nurses, therapists, psychologists, lawyers, and teachers and much more. God has equipped the church with all the necessary gifts that it will need to keep the church strong and healthy, but the church is not using what it has been given. The church has betrayed God and cannot continue with this type of mindset. The believer has been given all the gifts that it will need to fight the good fight.

There is a war that has been going on for a very long time, two worlds fighting against each other. Let's take a look at it through God's eyes. God our Father which art in heaven in heaven, hallowed be thy name. Thy kingdom come, thy will be done on earth, as it is in heaven. Here we have heaven coming against earth. We are to the Father as to the earth. Earth without heaven cannot exist. I say this because to balance earth heaven has to be present in the earth. That is, God has chosen to present heaven to earth that it would look like heaven. So, God has chosen certain people to anoint heaven upon them so that they would be able to preach and teach heaven. He chose individuals that would not betray Him or His kingdom or the laws of His kingdom.

God anointed and gifted certain people to carry heaven in them. It was Jesus and John the Baptist that said the Kingdom of heaven is at hand and the kingdom is in you, meaning the people. They did not understand and still today we do not understand. The church has rejected the teaching of the Kingdom of God. The teaching today has gone south. The church has to stop betraying the teaching of God and His kingdom. You would wonder why so many in the church are lost. The reason why is that the teaching is not correct. We have people teaching that should not be teaching, training, or discipling.

We have betrayed God in the discipling of His kingdom and that is the reason for the condition of the church. We must go back to the basic fundamentals that the Bible teaches, the blueprint that has already been established; and the foundation which has already been put in place. We must get back to foundation principles. We must fight the spirit of betrayal. We need to remember that we, the church, have the power in Jesus Christ!

Hatred. (Matthew 24:10) "And then shall many be offended, and shall betray one another, and shall hate one another." In this verse Jesus tells the disciples and those that are around that many will be offended because of hearing the truth. Many believers like to quote the verse which says, "and ye shall know the truth, and the truth shall make you free." (John 8:32) The truth is that many who quote the verse don't even believe what they are saying, because they have not been made free from the religious mind set. The true believer knows that they are going up against the enemy and that they are hated because they carry the truth. Jesus was preparing the disciples for what they would encounter when they went out preaching and teaching the word of God and His Kingdom. Jesus was teaching them of what they would encounter from non-believers and all who had hatred in their hearts and minds. The hatred of Jews from the Muslims and Romans has continued from back then to today; it has not changed. Today we have many other religions that are doing the same thing; this must stop! We must stop this hatred; all it does is keep us apart. We know better and we are giving the adversary the upper hand.

How does the government say one nation under God and yet does not say what God says? They pledge allegiance to the flag and lie about its pledge of allegiance to God. This shows that the government hates God and the people of God. How can God bless a nation that does not love Him in truth and in spirit? Let's look at some of the things the government is doing that are against the law of God. Ministers of God being arrested for evangelizing out in the street, killing babies through abortions, teaching that it's alright to be unidentified as a boy or a girl. This is hatred teaching the children that their true identity isn't worth anything. We should come together as one to fight against this agenda the devil has launched against our children. He is using the government to implement his agenda. It's time for the church to take her place out in the open. When the church stands up God will show up and show out in the church with power and His glory. The church has to fight against the spirit of hate.

Three predicted ill effects of persecution Matthew (24:10-12)

1. The apostasy of some. When the profession of Christianity begins to cost men dearly, then shall many be offended; they will begin to pick quarrels with their religion, grow weary of it, and at length revolt from it. Suffering times are shaking times, and some fall in the storm who stood in fair weather. They like their religion while they can have it cheap, but if their profession of faith costs them anything, they quit.

2. They shall betray one another. That is, those who have treacherously deserted their religion, shall hate and betray those who adhere to it. Apostates have commonly been the most bitter and violent persecutors.

3. The general declining and cooling of many. When the saints are hated, expect two things: (a) The abounding of iniquity, more extensive than ordinary, so that hell seems to have broken loose in blasphemies against God and enmities to the saints. (b) The abating of love, which is the consequence of the former. Or it may be understood more as brotherly love. When iniquity abounds, Christians begin to be shy and suspicious of one another, affections are alienated, distances created, parties made; and, thereby, love comes to nothing. (Matthew Henry's Commentaries) This is taking place right now. I believe that God is separating those that are for Him and His Kingdom. This is the truth that Jesus was prophesying about the last days and is still prophesying today.

False Prophets. (Matthew 24:11) "And many false prophets shall rise and deceive many." (Matthew 24:24) "For there shall arise false Christs, and false prophets, and shall shew great signs and wonders, insomuch that, if it were possible, they shall deceive the very elect." False prophets were in abundance in the heathen nations surrounding God's people. Their medium of revelation was divination and other occult practices as spoken of in Deuteronomy 18:1-14.

Deuteronomy 13:1-2 and Zechariah 13:2 had its greatest impetus in the time of the monarchy. Apostasy came in the kings of Israel and Judah. True prophets denounced the wicked kings, while these kings viewed the true prophets with suspicion and antagonism. False prophets arose who found it more convenient to be loyal to a corrupt king but disloyal to God. They prophesied for advantage and personal gain (see Micah 3:5-11). From the book *Understanding the Prophetic Ministry*, by Apostle Ruben A. Martinez, "You don't have to look too far, all you have to do is look at the governments of the world."

Government leaders are to be considered, in a very small way, prophets because they speak for the people. The U.S. has a president who represents a nation; this is the opposite of a king. We must wake up and ask God to open our eyes so we can clearly see what is going on right in our face. Governments were formed to protect the people not to rule them. In the book of Genesis 1: 26-28, it is very clear that God gave man dominion over what He created - the fish, vegetation, fowls of the air and the animals, and every creeping thing. If you know the word dominion, then you won't be surprised that dominion also has to do with a type of ruling over others. To rule over others does not mean that you go right out to kill them. If we are going to kill, let the church kill the evil spirits that are using other people to the will of the enemy, the devil and his imps. The devil has the church fighting against each other. This needs to stop! We must come together as one to fight the good fight. We must teach the word of God the right way.

The church must expose all the false prophets that are running around deceiving the church. Pastors must work with true Prophets and true Apostles. This is the foundation of the church. We can do this working together, it's the only way, and putting at the front of what God wants to do with His church. A prophet is one who speaks for another, or someone who lends his voice to another. The major purpose of these servants – prophets – was to declare God's heart to His people by piercing the hearts of His people, that they might return to His ways. From the book of *Understanding the Prophetic Ministry* by Prophet Ruben Martinez, "it is said when you see how blatant the government is and the church is with their lies, this does not go well with God." Let's see why Nineveh fell from the grace of God. The prophet Nahum refers to Nineveh as a "bloody city, full of lies and plunder" (Nahum 3:1) and describes its sins in more detail: "There is no end to the looting and plundering, murder and destruction." (Nahum 3:19) These verses paint a picture of a city that was characterized by corruption, greed, and violence. (gospel-focus.com) The question to ask is, is the United States following in the same pattern that Nineveh did. The church must know and understand that she is called out from among them, meaning to move away from the sin of the world and governments, and leaders of sin and lies. The church has the power to overthrow sin. The church must let the true prophets speak the will of God. True prophets must show up and speak the will of God. True prophets will speak the mind of God. Prophets cannot stay silent anymore! It is time for the true church of God to wake up and take its place.

Lawlessness Abounding. (Matthew 24:12-13) "And because iniquity shall abound, the love of many shall wax cold. But he that shall endure unto the end, the same shall be saved." Jesus reveals to us that lawlessness would abound toward the end, it is here now right in front of our faces.

Jesus tells us clearly that lawlessness will increase in the last days, and we are seeing this right in front of our eyes. We are seeing Matthew 24 playing out right now; what are we looking for? It's here; it's time to wake up and fight back now. The real church of the Lord Jesus Christ must get ready for the biggest fight it has ever had. The increase of the sin of lawlessness is here. The hearts that once burned with passion for God and others has grown cold. Many churches have grown cold, the pulpit has grown cold, and the teaching has grown cold. Many are leaving the church because the pastors have lost touch with God. The flock that God has given them cannot get a true word from the pastors. The church is not being prepared; what is going to take place?

This reminds me of the ten virgins, 5 were ready and the other 5 were not. In reading and studying Matthew 24 and all the prophecies that Jesus prophesied is all taking place right now. Many have taught that Matthew 24 is for the Jewish people, and not for everyone that studies the Bible to learn it and to apply it. Yes there are many prophecies that have yet to come to light, but on the other hand many have taken place, and many believers have not realized that the prophecies are being fulfilled. Many prophecies are not understood because there has not been clear teaching on how to understand prophecies. You can't understand what you don't know, and this happens because of bad teaching and bad doctrine. Matthew 24 is all about prophecies concerning the end of the times that we are experiencing right now. We are seeing what lawlessness does to a nation and to the nations of the world. Jesus said that this would take place! Can we stop what is taking place? If the governments of the world turn to God, I believe that God would repent of the judgment of the world.

Love Decreasing. (Matthew 24:12) "And because iniquity shall abound, the love of many shall wax cold." (2Timothy 3:1-2) "This, know also, that in the last days perilous times shall come. For men shall be lovers of their own selves, covetous, boasters, proud, blasphemers, disobedient to parents, unthankful, unholy, without natural affection, trucebreakers, false accusers, incontinent, fierce, despisers of those that are good…" So we see that these verses in 3Timothy are in play right now. One of the biggest questions for the church right now is whether she is going to teach what is taking place right now. Is the church going to wake up and get the heart of the Father? The church at this point is off course and must get back on course. Many leaders in the church need to get back in touch with the Holy Spirit and get revelation from God. I cannot say this any clearer that the church must wake up and prepare their congregants. The Bible is very clear on what it says and what it teaches. The prophecies in the Bible are very clear and to the point. The church can no longer ignore the prophetic voice of God. There are true prophets and there are false prophets. The church needs to get real; just as much as there are false prophets there are also false pastors that should not be in the pulpit.

The church has to love every word of God. Love is failing in the church and the church is failing itself. The last days are perilous times and that is not being taught in the church. Paul is teaching Timothy to prepare for the last days. Sin plays the biggest part in the last days. This is what Paul is saying in this chapter 3 of 2Timothy. Is the church going to prepare the people of God? How far and how long will the church go depends on how the leadership of the church moves. People have to run to God not from Him. Paul tells Timothy, "All scripture is given by inspiration of God, and is profitable for doctrine, for reproof, for correction, for instruction in righteousness: that the man of God may be perfect, thoroughly furnished unto all good works." (2Timothy 3:16-17) If we are not teaching this chapter in its fullness, then we are not teaching about the last days. The truth must be heard, and we must stand on the truth, not on the watered-down preaching and teaching that is going on today. The church has moved away from teaching the Kingdom of God. There are traitors in the kingdom, trucebreakers, false accusers, and despisers of those that are good.

The Kingdom and the Church: To understand the kingdom of God, we must realize that it is not the same thing as the church. The church is composed of those who have been redeemed through the death and resurrection of Jesus and who are called to expand His kingdom, just as Jesus did when he lived on the earth. (Guillermo Maldonado,

The Kingdom of power) The church is only mentioned twice in the Bible, but the Kingdom is mentioned over 100 times. So, will you love the kingdom or the church?

We are seeing ungodly men in the church and outside the church. The church must wake up and take control of what God has given the church. We have to see that we are in perilous times. The times that we are living in are dangerous with corruption in our own government, and even in the church. This is not good for the kingdom of God or for the world. (2Timothy 3:5) "Having a form of godliness, but denying the power thereof: from such turn away."

One has to study the Bible to have an understanding of end time revelation in order to discern what is going on right now. Ungodly men, anti-Christian and impostors are posing as God's representatives. Love has been decreasing in the church throughout the world. People have no respect for the meaning of love, let alone respect for the love of God. The love and the peace of God passes all under-standing of man. Looking for love in all the wrong places is the downfall of man, not looking for the love of God that transforms man. The love of God is very powerful; it gives life.

Increased Missionary Work. (Matthew 24:14) "And this gospel of the kingdom shall be preached in all the world for a witness unto all nations; and then shall the end come." We have heard so many things about the last days and that the end is near, but the reading of this verse, says the opposite of what is being prophesied today. There is a whole lot that has to take place for the end to come. That would mean that the Kingdom of God has been set up for Him to make His appearance. At this point I don't see it taking place right now.

Let's look at what the verse says. It says this gospel of the kingdom shall be preached in all the world for a witness unto all nations. This part of the verse has been completed! So, the church must not let itself be deceived by all of the false prophecies that are buzzing around like flies. The gospel must be preached and heard throughout the entire world and rejected by those who don't believe or are not willing to repent of their sins. God has been sending missionaries throughout the world and still does today. What I have noticed is that many who say they are missionaries, have not gone out on a missionary trip or been trained in the missionary work. Where there is no training there is no sending. Doing the work of a missionary takes a lot of learning. It's not an easy ministry. Real missionary work is when you are sent out into the field to get the harvest. When a person is sent out it's because they are ready. God never sends anyone out who is not prepared.

The church must begin to train congregants in their ministry. Before Jesus Christ can return, the foundation needs to be prepared. We cannot forget that there must be a great revival that has to take place. When Ekklesia (Church) begins to look like the kingdom of God then it will move the hand of God to release Jesus Christ. I believe that there is a whole lot that the church has to do before the second coming of Jesus Christ. I believe that the ministry of the Evangelist has to be more visible not just in the church, but also outside the church. Many claim to be an Evangelist, but yet they are not doing the work of an Evangelist.

Pastors also must be present outside of the church to see that those being sent out to do the work are doing it the right way. It is time for the church to come out from inside the walls of the building and take the church into the streets and present the Kingdom of God. Then we can say that the missionary work is being done in the communities that we live in. There are a lot of people that are hurting and are in need of help. The kingdom of God has everything that is needed to create change in a sick and dying world.

Governments around the world make changes every day. The question to ask is why the church isn't making changes also. The church has to counter what the governments are doing against the church. The church has to bring the church to governments and let them know that it does not stand alone, it needs the church. It should not be that the only time that the church sees them is when it's voting time. The governments must be held responsible for the changes they make that affect the world. No one is to be left out of the missionary field. The kingdom must also be presented to the governments of the world.

The Abomination of Desolation. (Matthew 24:15) "When ye therefore shall see the abomination of desolation, spoken of by Daniel the prophet, stand in the holy place, (whoso readeth, let him understand)"

(Daniel 9: 27) "And he shall confirm the covenant with many for one week: and in the midst of the week, he shall cause the sacrifice and the oblation to cease, and for the overspreading of abominations he shall make it desolate, even until the consummation, and that determined shall be poured upon the desolate." (2Thessalonians 2:4) "Who opposeth and exalteth himself above all that is called God, or that is worshiped; so that he as God sitteth in the temple of God, shewing himself that he is God."

Revelation 13

The Tabernacle is the first to be built and dedicated to God when they freed the Israelites from Egyptian slavery. It was built in the wilderness around 1450 BC. The temple was portable, so that wherever the Israelites went the Tabernacle went with them. This is the Tabernacle built by Moses.

The first Temple was built by King Solomon around 990-931BCE. It was completed 957BCE. After 440 years then the temple of Solomon superseded the Tabernacle in Jerusalem as the dwelling place of God. The second Temple was built during the time of Herod. The Babylonian army destroyed the First Temple, then the second Temple was destroyed by the Romans under the command of Titus. Let's now look at the building of third temple. It has not been built yet and we know that it will be built, but we do not know when. There is so much talk about the last days and no one seems to have an answer to what the last days are. So, to find out what the last are, we will look at the Bible and see what it says about the last days. Many are saying that we are at the end of the world, but I say no. We are at best coming to the end of a system. That would mean that the governments of the world are going to bring in a new system to govern the world. To know and to understand the last days we must study 2Timothy 3, Luke 21 and 2Thessalonians. God does not want the church to be caught off guard. So, before we come to the end of the world, let's wait for the third Temple to be built and for the Antichrist to be revealed. For those that have given a prophecy saying the end will come in 2025 or 2027, I have news for anyone who believes these false prophecies, they're in for a rude awakening. This is what the Bible says in the book of Matthew 24:36, "But of that day and hour knoweth no man, no, not the angels of heaven, but my father only."

(Mark 13:32) "But of that day and that hour knoweth no man, no not the angels which are in heaven, neither the Son, but the Father." Many are being deceived by all these false prophets that are popping up out of nowhere. This is the right time for the church to wake up and teach the true doctrine of God. This is a great time to pray and ask God to send the true prophets and the true apostles. The harvest is ripe to go out and get the fruit.

The new Jewish temple, V15, 26, Rev11:1-2, Dan 8: 9-13, 9:27 and 11:45 and 2Th 2:4.

The great tribulation of 31/2 v 21 Matt, 12:1, Rev12 1, 19:21.

Martyrdoms Matt 24:9, 22, Dan 8:24, Rev 7:9-17, 15:2-4 and 20:4-6.

Flight of the Jews from Judea v 16-21, Rev 12:6, 14, Is 16:1-5, Ps 60: 4-8, Dan 11: 40-45, Ez 20:33-38 and Hos 2:14-16.

Increased satanic powers Matt 24 :24, Th 2 :8-12, Rev13, 16:14 and 19-20.

Surfeiting Matt 24:38, Lk 17:28, 21:34.

Sex crimes Matt 24:38, Lk 17:27.

Procrastination and lethargy Matt v 39.

These are the 24 signs of the second coming of Jesus Christ that are found in the book of Matthew chapter 24. Jesus prophesied all these events that would take place in the last days before His second coming. This is the end time revelation. I would like for everyone who reads this book to recommend it and pass it on to others. Revelation comes through taking the time to study and get the heartbeat of the Father, the Son, and the Holy Spirit. The members that are supposed to make up the body of Christ have to be the bricks that are truly in unity with Jesus Christ. The church must hold itself accountable to what it knows and learn what it does not know. The Church needs to know and understand what end times means. When something ends it means that there is going to be something new that is going to come out. Everyone is talking about the reset that is coming or is here; and we don't understand what is taking place right now. It is all taking place right in our face right now. The world has changed in a lot of ways and we're seeing it. What will it take for the church to open her eyes? Jesus warned of these times concerning what would take place before His second coming. I strongly ask the church to pray and get the true understanding of the end time revelation that is right here in the time that we are in. Are we ready or are we unprepared for what is coming? I believe that the majority of the church is not prepared or ready to fight against the onslaught that is taking place right now and the one to come.

Previously Written Books

Out of the MIRY CLAY (2016)

The purpose of this book is to show the reader that God is no respecter of persons. God will find you right where you are and begin the work that He has already planned for your life. This book will show the believer and the non-believer that all things are possible with God.

Understanding the Prophetic Ministry (2021)

The need for the education of our prophets who are comprehensively trained is increasing. Prophets must obtain a firm biblical foundation along with their experiential training. This manual provides a firm foundation for prophets in training.

www.ingramcontent.com/pod-product-compliance
Lightning Source LLC
Chambersburg PA
CBHW030523100426
42813CB00001B/135